Malnutrition

Fitness
Food & Nutrition
Food Safety
Health & Hygiene
Healthy Diet
Malnutrition

Malnutrition

MASON CREST
PHILADELPHIA
MIAMI

Mason Crest
450 Parkway Drive, Suite D
Broomall, Pennsylvania 19008
(866) MCP-BOOK (toll-free)
www.masoncrest.com

First printing
9 8 7 6 5 4 3 2 1

ISBN (hardback) 978-1-4222-4223-0
ISBN (series) 978-1-4222-4217-9
ISBN (ebook) 978-1-4222-7594-8

Cataloging-in-Publication Data on file with the Library of Congress

Developed and Produced by National Highlights, Inc.
Interior and Cover Design: Jana Rade
Copy Editor: Adirondack Editing
Production: Michelle Luke

QR CODES AND LINKS TO THIRD-PARTY CONTENT

CONTENTS

KEY ICONS TO LOOK FOR

 WORDS TO UNDERSTAND: These words with their easy-to-understand definitions will increase the reader's understanding of the text while building vocabulary skills.

 SIDEBARS: This boxed material within the main text allows readers to build knowledge, gain insights, explore possibilities, and broaden their perspectives by weaving together additional information to provide realistic and holistic perspectives.

 EDUCATIONAL VIDEOS: Readers can view videos by scanning our QR codes, providing them with additional educational content to supplement the text. Examples include news coverage, moments in history, speeches, iconic sports moments, and much more!

 TEXT-DEPENDENT QUESTIONS: These questions send the reader back to the text for more careful attention to the evidence presented there.

 RESEARCH PROJECTS: Readers are pointed toward areas of further inquiry connected to each chapter. Suggestions are provided for projects that encourage deeper research and analysis.

 SERIES GLOSSARY OF KEY TERMS: This back-of-the-book glossary contains terminology used throughout this series. Words found here increase the reader's ability to read and comprehend higher-level books and articles in this field.

OVERVIEW

GOOD NUTRITION

Elements of good nutrition include:

- Consuming food and nutrients needed for energy and growth
- Eating a balanced diet
- Good nutrition encourages:
  - Development, growth, and maintenance of tissues and cells
  - Improved immune system, leading to less illness
  - Production of energy for warmth and movement

ESSENTIAL NUTRIENTS

- Macronutrients
- Carbohydrates
- Fats (lipids)
- Proteins
- Micronutrients
- Vitamins
- Minerals
- Water

 WORDS TO UNDERSTAND

COMMUNICABLE: something, such as a disease, that can be passed on to someone else

MACRONUTRIENTS: nutrients that are needed in substantial quantities

MICRONUTRIENTS: nutrients that are needed by the body in small quantities (but are still vital for health)

MACRONUTRIENTS: CARBOHYDRATES

- Energy-giving foods composed of starch and sugars
- Common staple foods eaten regularly and accounting for up to 80 percent of the diet in developing countries
- Quickly absorbed by the body
- Sources
  - Cereals (millet, sorghum, maize, rice)
  - Root crops (cassava, potatoes)
  - Starchy fruits (bananas)

MACRONUTRIENTS: FATS AND OILS (LIPIDS)

- Energy-giving foods
- Not produced by the body
- Absorbed more slowly than carbohydrates
- Account for small part of diet in developing countries
- Fats (solids): Butter, ghee, lard, margarine
- Oils (liquids): Corn oil, soybean oil, peanut oil

MICRONUTRIENTS: MINERALS

- Inorganic compounds not synthesized by the body
- Needed in very small quantities but essential
- Important for biochemical processes and formation of cells and tissues
- Sources: plants and animal products
- Energy requirements:
  - Energy is needed to maintain health, growth, and appropriate physical activity
  - Energy needs vary based on age, gender, and activity level
- Met through an age-appropriate balanced diet based on:
  - Basal metabolism: energy needed for basic body functions
  - Metabolic response to food: energy needed to digest, absorb, and utilize food
  - Physical activity: work, rest, and play
  - Physiology: pregnancy, lactation, and maturation increase energy needs

WATER

- Main component of the body (60 percent of body mass)
- Needed for digestion, absorption and other body functions
- Regularly lost through sweating, excretion, and breathing
- The advice to drink 8 cups of water (1.9 liters) of water per day is very general, but is probably a good guideline for the average person. However, needs can vary.
- A more exact amount needed each day is the following: 11.5 cups (2.7 liters) for women and 15.5 cups (3.7 liters) for men. This includes water that you get from foods, which is typically about 20 percent of overall intake.

CONDITIONS ASSOCIATED WITH UNDERNUTRITION AND OVERNUTRITION

- Scurvy (lack of Vitamin C)
- Rickets (lack of Vitamin D)
- Mental, adrenal disorders (lack of B Vitamins)
- Mineral deficiency
- Osteoporosis (lack of calcium in older people)
- Diet-related non **communicable** diseases
- Diabetes
- Coronary heart disease
- Obesity
- High blood pressure

WHAT IS MALNUTRITION?

The condition that arises when there is either a **deficiency** or an excess of nutrients in the body is called malnutrition. It is a medical condition in which health cannot be restored through diet control alone. Proper medical treatment is required to deal with malnutrition. An unbalanced diet may lead to many deficiencies in our body. These deficiencies can cause a number of diseases, some of which may even have a lifelong impact. Although we associate malnutrition with a severe lack of food, excess intake of certain nutrients can also result in nutrition disorders.

 WORDS TO UNDERSTAND

DEFICIENCY: less of something than is needed

DETRIMENTAL: harmful

SUSCEPTIBLE: prone or likely to

UNDERNUTRITION

Undernutrition, or subnutrition, is a deficiency of essential nutrients in the body. It can occur due to lack of food, lack of nutrients in the food, or by the body's inability to use the provided nutrients. In all cases, the body suffers from weakness and disorders related to nutrition. The lack of proper nutrition affects the growth and development of the body. Undernutrition, in general, is the result of unhealthy or poor diets due to poverty. It is the most common reason for malnutrition in the world.

AGE GROUPS AND MALNUTRITION

Children are especially **susceptible** to malnutrition, as their growth and development suffers the most from nutrient deficiency. The elderly may also suffer from malnutrition. Our body stops producing certain nutrients in old age. These nutrients must be supplied through diet.

OVERNUTRITION

Overnutrition is the state of having an excess of nutrients. Many people believe that only the deficiency of nutrients can be harmful for our body. However, exceeding the normal requirement of nutrients may also cause problems. Our body needs the essential nutrients in balanced quantities. Overnutrition can be caused by the inclusion of limited nutrients in our diet.

This video will give you a quick overview of the issue of malnutrition.

However, malnutrition cases caused by undernutrition are far more numerous than those caused by overnutrition.

ATTITUDE TOWARD MALNUTRITION

Many people fail to understand the importance of proper nutrition. They don't even try to make necessary changes in their diet. This attitude is the main reason behind many cases of malnutrition. Lack of knowledge about malnutrition is common among both educated and uneducated people. An indifferent attitude toward our own essential nutrition can prove **detrimental** in the long run, even if it doesn't cause any immediate harm.

DID YOU KNOW?

- Dairy products contain lactose, a type of sugar that is difficult for some people to digest.
- Stunted growth is an important symptom of chronic malnutrition.

HOW TO PREVENT MALNUTRITION

According to the World Health Organization (WHO), the largest contributor to global child mortality is malnutrition. In fact, even in developed countries, a surprising number of people across age groups suffer from malnutrition. However, many disorders and health conditions caused by malnutrition can be easily prevented by taking proper **precautions**. Most nutrition disorders can be avoided by adopting healthy eating practices and staying alert to potential problems.

 WORDS TO UNDERSTAND

DETECTION: uncovering of facts or information

PRECAUTIONS: safeguards; plans designed to prevent an undesirable outcome

PROMPTLY: swiftly

BALANCED DIET

Malnutrition is primarily caused by any increase or decrease in the quantity of required nutrients. This imbalance can be treated by switching to a balanced diet. Protein deficiency is very common in disorders related to malnutrition. Health conditions may also be caused by an unbalanced intake of vitamins, minerals, and other essential nutrients. All you need is a balanced diet that supplies your body with nourishment in the required quantities. However, a balanced diet alone is no guarantee against all diseases.

DEALING WITH THE CAUSES

Malnutrition can have several causes. Poverty and food scarcity are the causes of malnutrition that are most difficult to deal with. Other problems like medical conditions, physical problems, and poor diets also call for attention. Efforts are being made by governments across the world to deal with these causes effectively.

BREASTFEEDING

The ideal way of providing nutrition to newborns is breastfeeding, which helps in building a healthy body and also strengthens a child's **immune system**. This reduces the chances and cases of malnutrition. It is important to note that mothers should also take care of their own nourishment during the breastfeeding period.

KNOWLEDGE

Proper information and knowledge about malnutrition can save us from its ill effects. Educating people on the health effects of malnutrition can help in preventing it to some extent. Nowadays, many schools and colleges have included malnutrition in their course content for the purpose of spreading awareness.

IDENTIFYING SYMPTOMS

Early **detection** of any health problem makes its cure easier. This holds true for all diseases, including those caused by malnutrition. The most common symptom of malnutrition is weight loss. Joint pains, low energy levels, fatigue, and brittle nails are also common symptoms of malnutrition. In some cases, slow healing of wounds can also indicate the incidence of malnutrition. Therefore, it is advisable to identify these symptoms as soon as they occur and deal with them **promptly**.

DID YOU KNOW?

- There are more than 462 million underweight people in the world.
- According to the WHO, malnutrition in childhood results in lower educational achievement during adulthood.

WHAT CAUSES MALNUTRITION?

Food and nutrition are directly related to each other. Lack of a balanced diet can lead to different nutritional disorders. Malnutrition can be caused by many factors, some of which may directly lead to this condition. However, some factors are indirectly responsible for malnutrition. The physical, social, and economic conditions of a country may create a general atmosphere of scarcity that can become a possible cause of malnutrition. Common causes of malnutrition are poor diet, medical problems, poverty, food scarcity, and certain physical factors.

WORDS TO UNDERSTAND

APPETITE: the desire and ability to consume food

CALAMITIES: accidents or disasters that cause large-scale damage

ROUTINELY: regularly, as a habit

POOR DIET

Our nutrition is completely determined by the foods we eat. Any imbalance in the quantity of nutrients in our diet directly affects the nourishment of our body. Personal attitude plays a very important role in developing diet habits. People who **routinely** choose taste over nutrition may choose poor or unhealthy diets. Many people are unwilling to change their diet to suit their nutritional requirements. Such an attitude is hazardous to health.

MEDICAL PROBLEMS

Diseases and infections in our body may affect its capacity to absorb nutrients. They can also have a direct effect on our food requirements. Some medical conditions affect the **appetite**. Diarrhea, vomiting, digestive problems, and eating disorders are some common medical conditions that affect our food intake. However, mental health can also affect our nutrition. In depression or disturbed mental conditions, people lose their appetite. They may also develop unusual food habits that are unhealthy.

POVERTY

Our purchasing power directly affects our capacity to afford healthy diets. Poverty is the reason so many people can't afford to eat nutritious food. Due to rising prices of food items, poor people are increasingly facing problems because they chose food items based on price. As such, nutrition is not their primary concern when making food choices. Most recorded cases of malnutrition are among those affected by poverty.

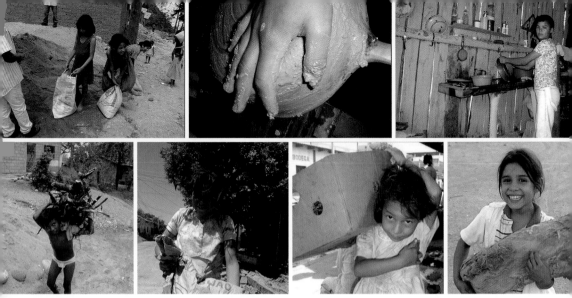

FOOD SCARCITY

World food shortage is another major contributor to the rise of malnutrition. Natural calamities, agricultural problems, and food spoilage are the main causes of food shortages around the world. The quality of food is also affected by contamination. Both the quantity and quality of food are important for nutrition. Together, these problems affect people's diets and lead to nutritional disorders such as malnutrition.

PHYSICAL FACTORS

Many physical factors can also be responsible for poor nutrition of our body. Problems in chewing or swallowing food force people to change their food habits, so they sometimes switch to foods that are easier to eat even though they may not be very healthy. The dislike for certain food items due to their smell or taste also affects the balance of our diet.

 DID YOU KNOW?

- More than 800 million people worldwide suffer from malnutrition and hunger.
- Around three million children die from malnutrition every year.

DIAGNOSIS AND TREATMENT

A disease can be cured only if it is properly diagnosed. Nutritional **assessment** *is crucial to determining malnutrition cases. Proper diagnosis helps in detecting the reasons behind a nutritional disorder and the specific deficiency that has led to it. Treatments are effective only if the diagnosis is correct.*

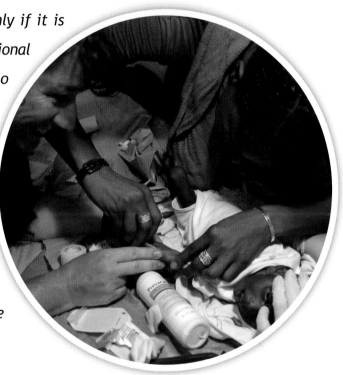

 ## WORDS TO UNDERSTAND

ASSESSMENT: evaluation

DIETICIAN: an expert on human diet and nutrition

ENTERAL: something (medication or nutrients) that passes through the intestine

PARENTERAL: something taken into the body through a route other than the intestines, such as through the bloodstream

METHODS TO DIAGNOSE MALNUTRITION

The Malnutrition Universal Screening Tool (MUST) is the most commonly used method for diagnosing malnutrition, and is primarily used in diagnosing malnutrition in adults or the elderly. This method involves a five-step plan for diagnosis. These steps include measuring height and weight, observing any unusual change in the same, diagnosing any existing diseases, determining the risk of malnutrition, and providing proper treatment.

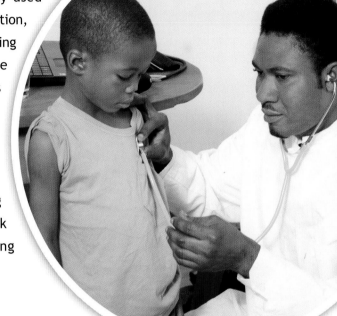

DIET METHOD

Many cases of malnutrition can be addressed by working with a **dietician** to improve the patient's diet. The dietician talks to the patient about his or her existing diet habits and the required changes. All individuals have their own nutritional requirements. The dietician makes the patient aware of these requirements and prepares a diet plan that will meet them. Additional nutrients can also be suggested.

ARTIFICIAL NUTRITIONAL SUPPORT METHOD

In serious cases of malnutrition, artificial nutritional support may be needed, which basically includes two methods: the **enteral** method and the **parenteral** feeding method. The enteral method is also known as the tube-feeding method. A tube is used to feed nutrients to patients that are unable to chew and swallow food in the usual way. In the parenteral method, a nutrient-rich liquid is directly administered into the veins of the patient.

MEDICINAL TREATMENT

There are some cases where malnutrition in children is not caused by the lack of a healthy diet, but due to cystic fibrosis—a condition in which the lungs and the digestive system become clogged with a sticky mucus, making it difficult for the body to digest food. In such cases, oral medicines are administered to the child to clear the digestive system. In some severe cases, malnourished children are rehydrated instead of immediately being given a nutrient-rich diet.

TREATING MALNUTRITION

The treatment for malnutrition is determined by a number of factors, such as the extent of malnourishment, the underlying causes of malnutrition, and the digestive ability of the patient. If at an early stage, malnutrition can be cured by diet correction and proper care. The main methods of treating malnutrition are diet supervision and artificial nutritional support. In some cases, certain medicines must be administered. Proper monitoring is important in all the methods.

 DID YOU KNOW?

- A habit of washing hands before meals can help prevent illnesses.
- Iodine deficiency affects more than two billion people worldwide.

EFFECTS OF MALNUTRITION

Malnutrition can have many negative effects on health, some of which may be physical, while others may be psychological. Malnutrition disrupts our growth and development, affecting mainly our height, weight, and organs. Our body's blood and tissues may also be affected by imbalanced nourishment. Some other common effects of malnutrition are deficiency diseases include low immunity, slow healing of wounds, reduced learning ability, and death.

WORDS TO UNDERSTAND

IMMUNITY: the body's ability to fight off illness and infection

METABOLIC: relating to the bodily processes needed to sustain life

LOW IMMUNITY

Nutrients play an extremely important role in guarding one's body against various diseases. They help in maintaining and increasing the body's immunity. The lack of required nutrients makes the body vulnerable to diseases and infections. In some cases, malnutrition can lead to serious diseases such as cancer, organ failure, and **metabolic** problems.

DEFICIENCY DISEASES

Malnutrition is caused by a disturbed balance of nutrients in one's diet, and this deficiency of the nutrients required by the body can cause additional disorders. Problems mainly occur due to an imbalance of nutrients such as calcium, iron, vitamins A, C, D, and B complex, and proteins. Common malnutrition diseases are kwashiorkor, marasmus, anemia, scurvy, and rickets. Diseases caused by malnutrition have greatly affected the growth of children around the world. Therefore, it is important for parents to ensure that their children are well-nourished.

REDUCED LEARNING ABILITY

A long-term effect of malnutrition is reduced learning ability. In some cases, the ability to remember or process information is adversely affected. This problem occurs mostly in children. Lack of important nutrients reduces the mind's ability to retain information.

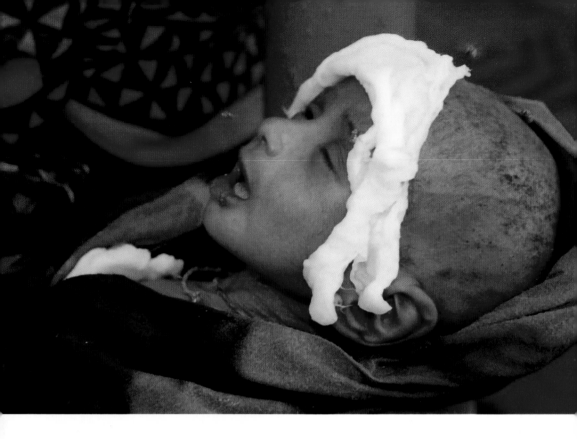

SLOW HEALING OF WOUNDS

Those who suffer from malnutrition experience slow healing of their wounds. In both overnutrition and undernutrition, wounds don't heal at the normal pace. Improper amounts of vitamins, proteins, and carbohydrates are responsible for reducing the body's healing ability. This increases the risk of other infections and affects the body's capacity to respond to treatments. Less oxygen in the body's tissues also affects the healing process.

 DID YOU KNOW?

- The most preventable cause of blindness in children is Vitamin A deficiency.
- Undernutrition in pregnant women can cause problems in their pregnancies.

HUNGER

Hunger is one of humanity's biggest and oldest problems. It is common to see people starving and dying of hunger in many parts of the world. However, it is safe to say that most of the world's hunger problems are concentrated in the developing and poorer countries. Economic challenges and storage problems deserve special attention to deal with the problem of hunger.

 WORDS TO UNDERSTAND

DEPRIVED: disadvantaged
FOOD INSECURE: describes the state of not having consistent access to food
ONEROUS: very difficult

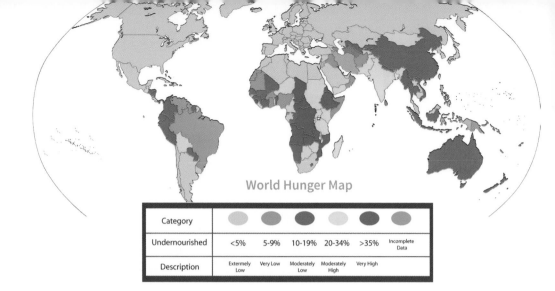

World Hunger Map

Category						
Undernourished	<5%	5-9%	10-19%	20-34%	>35%	Incomplete Data
Description	Extermely Low	Very Low	Moderately Low	Moderately High	Very High	

HUNGER IN ASIAN COUNTRIES

The problem of hunger is very common in some countries of Asia. More than 12 states in India show alarming levels of hunger. According to reports, more than 200 million people in India alone suffer from hunger problems. Other countries like Bangladesh, Pakistan, Sri Lanka, and China are also dealing with problems associated with hunger. Increased food production and proper water supply are required to improve conditions in these countries. Only then can the problem of hunger be tackled.

HUNGER IN AFRICAN COUNTRIES

Food problems in African countries are increasing at a frightening pace due to poverty and other economic problems, as well as multiple regional and civil wars. Approximately one-quarter of the people on the continent suffer from **food insecurity**. Some severely affected countries include the Congo, Burundi, Eritrea, Sierra Leone, Chad, and Ethiopia.

HUNGER IN LATIN AMERICAN COUNTRIES

The nations of Latin America are also facing hunger-related problems. Many political and economic reasons are responsible for this condition. Latin American countries are believed to have the greatest gap between rich and poor worldwide. Poor citizens in these countries find it **onerous** to afford food. Argentina, Venezuela, Columbia, and Peru are some Latin American countries that face hunger problems.

This video is about the issue of global hunger.

HUNGER WEAKENS ECONOMIC DEVELOPMENT

Basic human needs must be fulfilled for proper functioning of the body. An undernourished person cannot be expected to be able to perform well in any field. In the state of hunger, people are unable to work or even understand basic things properly. Healthy individuals can help their country to prosper economically with their active participation in its development. On the other hand, hunger hampers economic growth and development.

HOW TO OVERCOME HUNGER

Government agencies must be more active in solving this problem. Their efforts can start with an attempt to control the causes of hunger. There are countries where the food produced goes to waste due to the lack of storage facilities, instead of reaching the **deprived** sections of society. Every government should ensure that such waste is avoided.

 DID YOU KNOW?

- Malnourished children can spend as much as 160 days per year being sick.
- According to the World Hunger Education Service, nearly 100 million children under the age of five are underweight.

HUNGER AND THE ELDERLY

Old age can be a difficult period, particularly for those who lack financial stability. The elderly face many hunger-related problems. However, poverty is not the only reason for nutritional problems. The process of aging and increasing disturbances in health also affect their nutrition.

WORDS TO UNDERSTAND

CHRONIC: persistent

COMPOSITION: makeup

HORMONAL: relating to the hormones, substances in the body that regulate its functioning

CHANGES IN APPETITE

The body goes through several changes during old age. The appetite of some elderly people may become very low, which can lead to weight loss. This happens due to certain **hormonal** changes in the body. However, in some cases, their appetite can also increase, which can be a result of high physical activity, stress, and medication.

FOOD INSECURITY

The elderly also face food insecurities. Economic and noneconomic factors, such as household **composition**, income, race, and location are important for understanding food insecurity. However, money plays the most important role among all other factors. Food insecurity increases when elderly people live alone and there is no one to provide for them on a regular basis.

FACTORS AFFECTING FOOD REQUIREMENTS OF THE ELDERLY

The food requirements of the elderly are governed by many factors, including the body's functional problems, and reduction in the ability to regulate energy. These factors deeply effect the psychology of the elderly. Older people can fall into depression if they suffer from health problems, which in turn can affect their appetite, and they may experience a decline in the urge to eat.

HEALTH EFFECTS

The food problems faced by the elderly give rise to many health problems. The body becomes weak during old age and needs nourishment and maintenance. Poverty impedes the ability to provide for oneself. The health problems caused by hunger also go untreated in some cases due to a lack of finances. Old age can invite many diseases, even when hunger is not a problem. Deficiency diseases and chronic health problems are more common in old age.

PROTECTING THE FOOD NEEDS OF THE ELDERLY

Many efforts have being taken by government agencies and social service centers worldwide for the betterment of old people. Many health programs like elderly nutrition programs, child and adult care food programs, and others have been developed for helping the elderly. However, increasing the participation of older people in such programs is important if they are to be truly helped through such activities.

DID YOU KNOW?

- More than 25 million Americans aged 60 and over live at or below poverty level.
- The elderly are more susceptible to health conditions that result in malnutrition.

RIGHT TO FOOD

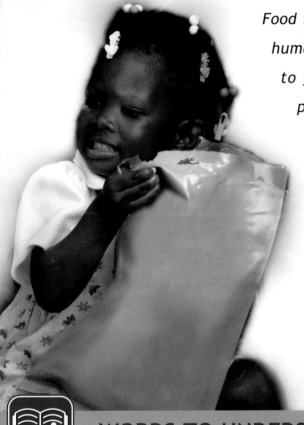

Food is a basic requirement of all human beings. Hence, the right to food is considered by many people to be a fundamental right. Every person should be provided with food in order to prevent hunger. People work and earn money to meet their food requirements. However, there are some people who are unable to earn enough money to provide for their meals.

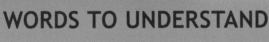

WORDS TO UNDERSTAND

FUNDAMENTAL: basic, essential

HINDRANCE: obstacle

HUMANITARIAN: related to human values and betterment of humankind

HUMAN NEEDS & FOOD RIGHTS

The idea of food rights emerged from the fact that food is a basic human need. There are three main goals behind the right-to-food program: respect, protect, and fulfill. In this context, "respect" means that the requirement for food must be respected and people should not be prevented from having food. The motive to "protect" states that the government and development agencies should protect the food needs of people. To "fulfill" this right, efforts must be made by governments across the world to strengthen people's access to food.

RIGHT TO FOOD: MISCONCEPTIONS

People often misunderstand the right to food, assuming that it means they have the right to get food without any effort. This is incorrect. The right to food stipulates that we have the right to feed ourselves in a sufficient and dignified way, not that the government is expected to hand out free food to everyone. In some cases, help is provided to people who are unable to meet their food needs due to uncontrollable reasons.

WHY ARE FOOD RIGHTS IMPORTANT?

Food rights are important for many reasons. They help in the fulfillment and safety of human rights and needs. The right to food is more important for people living in developing countries, because hunger problems are more common in developing countries. Hunger problems can be solved more effectively with the help of food rights.

LEGAL STATUS OF FOOD RIGHTS

The right to have access to food is supported mainly by international human rights and **humanitarian** law. In 1948, the right to food was given acceptance internationally in the "Universal Declaration of Human Rights." Many other international, national, and regional authorities also support the right to food. There are many nonlegal declarations and guidelines that support right to food but are not legally enforceable.

OBSTACLES TO FOOD RIGHTS

There are many countries in the world that recognize the right to food but have not developed constitutional provisions to provide it with a legal framework. Another **hindrance** is that food security usually focuses on public policy goals and principles instead of the collective or individual right to food. This causes difficulties in implementing the right to food, as there is a lack of legal framework to ensure that it is followed in letter and spirit.

DID YOU KNOW?

- The right to food is part of the International Covenant in Economic, Social and Cultural Rights.
- According to estimates, around 800 million people suffer from hunger and malnutrition.

STARVATION

Starvation is caused by the extreme lack of nutrients in the body. It can also be understood as an extreme form of malnutrition. Proper medication and treatment is required for improving the condition and the health of starved individuals. Extreme starvation can even result in death.

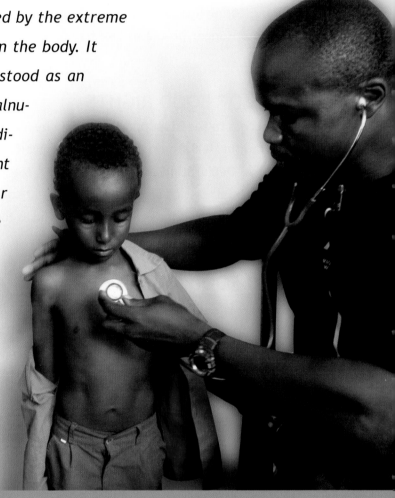

 WORDS TO UNDERSTAND

ABSORPTION: soaking up

DEHYDRATION: a lack of water in the body

IMPLEMENTATION: the process of putting a plan or policy into effect

CAUSES

People who are unable to eat because they can't afford it are the main victims of starvation. Wars, famines, and many other natural disasters can create conditions where people must face the shortage of both food and money. Many are forced to starve in such situations. Besides the lack of food, certain bodily disorders can make the **absorption** of nutrients difficult for the body. This condition can also lead to starvation.

SYMPTOMS

The most common and easily visible symptom of starvation is excessive weight loss. Deficiency diseases are also signs of starvation. During this condition, the stomach becomes sensitive and fails to feel hunger and thirst. This tendency also leads to **dehydration** in some cases. Energy levels also drop and the entire body looks weak and pale.

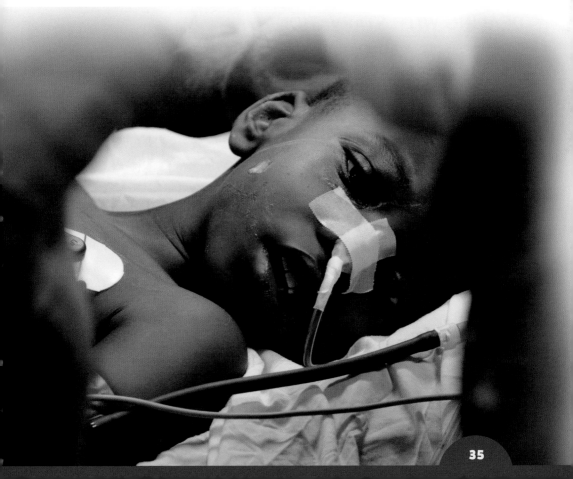

STARVATION IN DEVELOPING COUNTRIES

Food problems are common in many parts of the world. However, developing countries face more problems related to food and hunger than the developed world. Starvation is also more common among people in developing countries; since people living in developing countries suffer more poverty, they are less likely to be able to meet their food requirements. Lack of adequate health facilities add to their woes, as they are unable to cure the medical causes of starvation.

EFFECTS

Starvation can have severe effects on our health. A starved body becomes susceptible to a number of diseases as the body's immunity becomes extremely low. This condition can also lead to organ failures. In severe cases, the victim of starvation may even die. Starvation not only has physical effects, but the economic and social development of a starved person are also adversely affected.

DEALING WITH STARVATION

Governments play a major role in dealing with the large-scale problem of starvation. They are responsible for policy formulation and its **implementation**. Those who can't afford food should benefit from various schemes designed by the government to grant them access to food. Food problems should be given special attention and sincere efforts should be made to deal with them. Those with medical conditions should consult a doctor.

DID YOU KNOW?

- According to one estimate, as many as a billion people suffer from hunger.
- Africa suffers from major starvation problems due to serious famines and droughts.

FOOD SYSTEMS

All the activities involved in producing, processing, transporting, storing, selling, and eating food can be grouped together as a "food system." Every country has its own food system. Various methods and practices are involved in different food activities. This leads to a variety in food systems as well. Some common types of food systems are organic, local, and conventional food systems. Social, economic, political, and environmental factors greatly influence food systems.

 WORDS TO UNDERSTAND

CONVENTIONAL: describes an expected or usual way of doing things

DIVERSE: describes something with a lot of variety

FLEXIBILITY: how adaptable something is

Find out more about food systems.

A HEALTHY FOOD SYSTEM: PRINCIPLES

There are many principles that help in maintaining a healthy food system. A good food system takes care of the health of the farmers who produce the food, the people who consume it, and even the workers involved in its packaging. It should carefully use natural resources. It should aim at providing affordable food, and it should be economically balanced. A good food system is also diverse and transparent in nature. The **flexibility** to respond to emergency situations is also a feature of healthy food systems.

FOOD SYSTEM ACTIVITIES

All food systems have certain activities in common: production, processing, packaging and distribution, retailing, and consumption. Production involves many activities like obtaining land, labor, and raw materials, planting crops, and harvesting. Processing involves activities related to transforming agricultural products into finished goods. Packaging and distribution deal with the maintenance of food quality, appearance, and regulations. Retailing and consumption deal with the organization and functioning of markets.

CONVENTIONAL FOOD SYSTEMS

Conventional food systems are based on the principles of maximum efficiency and low costs. Cheap fossil fuels are used in many activities of this food system. In a conventional food system, foods are prepared using basic ingredients. They are cooked when mealtime is near. Since it aims at reducing costs and increasing output, this system may operate at the expense of regional and global ecosystems, due to its creation of pollution and greenhouse gases.

LOCAL FOOD SYSTEMS

The food systems developed with locally available resources and products in mind are known as local food systems. These food systems are directly accessible to people nearby, and they aim at reducing geographical separation between the producer and the consumer. The problem of distances and transportation are thus reduced in this type of food system. Community-supported agriculture and farmers' markets are two examples.

ORGANIC FOOD SYSTEMS

The type of food system that tries to avoid the use of chemicals and its related products can be described as an organic food system. The organic food system involves natural ways of producing food. Pesticides and fertilizers are avoided in organic farming. Antibiotics and growth hormones are avoided in the rearing of livestock. Organic food systems are believed to consume less energy than the nonorganic food systems.

DID YOU KNOW?

- Around 9 percent of greenhouse gas emissions in the United States are caused by agricultural activities.
- California's food system has more than 700 certified farmers' markets.

DISEASES CAUSED BY MALNUTRITION

There are many diseases associated with malnutrition. Malnutrition reduces the body's energy levels, which affects our growth, development, and maintenance. All body parts are directly or indirectly affected in this condition. Malnutrition can be of two types: primary malnutrition or secondary malnutrition. Different diseases occur in both types of malnutrition.

 WORDS TO UNDERSTAND

ANEMIA: a blood condition often caused by a lack of iron or Vitamin B12

INSUFFICIENT: inadequate

RICKETS: a bone condition caused by a lack of Vitamin D

SCURVY: a disease caused by a lack of Vitamin C

PRIMARY MALNUTRITION

The state of malnutrition that is caused by an **insufficient** intake of food and nutrients is known as primary malnutrition. In some cases, people are forced to live without food either due to its unavailability or their inability to purchase it. Poverty and food shortage are the main reasons behind primary malnutrition. Starvation can be seen as a form of primary malnutrition. However, poor appetite can also lead to primary malnutrition in some cases.

SECONDARY MALNUTRITION

When the body is unable to absorb essential nutrients despite sufficient dietary intake, this is known as secondary malnutrition. Some people consume sufficient food, but their body fails to absorb nutrients from their meals. This becomes a major reason for secondary malnutrition. Diarrhea, parasitic infections, measles, and metabolic disturbances caused by surgery are some of the medical conditions that can lead to secondary malnutrition.

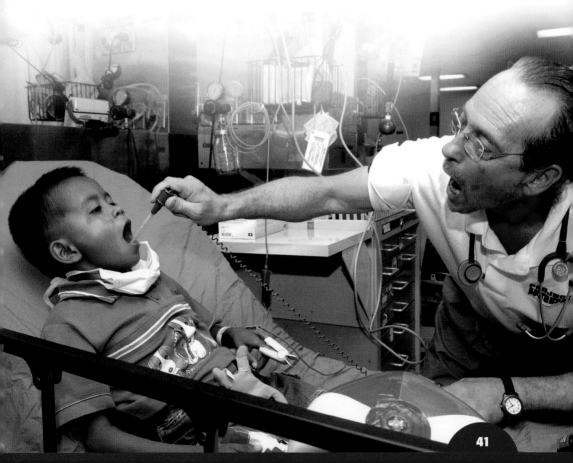

OTHER FORMS OF MALNUTRITION

Several nutrients are required for proper growth, development, and functioning of the body. Although there are some nutrients that are more important than others, the deficiency of any nutrient can hamper the functioning of our body. It must be remembered that those who look frail or weak are not the only ones to suffer from malnutrition. At times, even healthy-looking people lack balanced nourishment. Two additional forms of malnutrition are protein-energy malnutrition and micronutrient malnutrition.

MICRONUTRIENT MALNUTRITION

Micronutrient malnutrition is caused by the deficiency of essential vitamins and minerals. The deficiency may be caused by low intake of, or the body's failure to absorb, nutrients.

Some of the nutrients required by the body are iron, calcium, iodine, Vitamins A, D, and B12, zinc, folate, and selenium. These nutrients are required in small quantities regularly. **Anemia**, **rickets**, and **scurvy** are just some of the diseases caused by micronutrient malnutrition.

PROTEIN-ENERGY MALNUTRITION

As the name clearly indicates, protein-energy malnutrition is caused by an insufficient amount of protein in the diet. This deficiency can occur due to poor diet or an inability to absorb protein due to some medical condition. Protein-energy malnutrition can have serious health effects and may sometimes require complicated treatment. This form of malnutrition is more common in developing countries.

 DID YOU KNOW?

- Malnutrition is sometimes known as "hidden hunger."
- Zinc is a mineral required by our body for the proper functioning of the immune system. It also helps in the healing of wounds.

KWASHIORKOR

Kwashiorkor is one of the most common diseases caused by protein-energy malnutrition. Protein—a macronutrient—is very important for our body. Therefore, this disease can also be described as macronutrient deficiency disease.

Only a severe deficiency of protein can lead to this condition. Generally, it is children who suffer from kwashiorkor. More cases of kwashiorkor can be found in developing countries since children in these countries are given a diet low in proteins and high in carbohydrates.

 WORDS TO UNDERSTAND

IMPAIRMENT: handicap

SANITATION: community practices that encourage cleanliness

UNDERPRIVILEGED: describes someone with a below-average standard of living

CAUSES

Economic conditions and poverty play a very important role in creating the conditions for the development of kwashiorkor. Developing countries or places with limited food supply face many food problems. Natural disasters and famines also increase the incidences of kwashiorkor, as do poor knowledge about food and diet.

SYMPTOMS

The symptoms of kwashiorkor show up over time. They are visible in almost all cases of this disease. Some common symptoms are diarrhea, tiredness, rashes, swelling, irritation, and changes in skin and hair color. In some cases, body mass and muscles are also reduced from their normal size. Lack of growth and weight gain are also signs of kwashiorkor. In some cases of kwashiorkor, the belly protrudes in an unusual manner.

PREVENTION

Kwashiorkor can be prevented by making changes in the diet. A diet rich in carbohydrates and proteins is the first step toward preventing this disease. Safe water and **sanitation** are equally important. Governments should make efforts to help the **underprivileged** sections of society, since they are most susceptible to not only kwashiorkor but also other diseases caused by malnutrition. Food benefits should be provided to the poor so that their children can get proper nourishment.

EFFECTS

Kwashiorkor can have many ill effects on health. The body can become unshapely due to stomach enlargement. The skin and hair become dry and pale. Since protein is important for body growth, the condition of kwashiorkor can interfere with normal physical growth. The liver is also negatively affected in many cases. Serious cases can also lead to mental **impairment**. There is always a chance of relapse, even after treatment.

TREATMENT

Treatment begins with rehydration. Protein and calories are included in the diet for curing kwashiorkor. Dietary changes begin with including carbohydrates, fats, and simple sugars. Proteins are given at a later stage. Those affected by kwashiorkor from a lack of food are given food in small quantities so that their body can adapt to it. The intake of vitamins and minerals is also important in treating this disease.

 DID YOU KNOW?

- The first case of kwashiorkor was discovered in Ghana in 1930; the name comes from the language of the people who live there.
- Protein deficiency also affects a large number of elderly people, although they generally don't develop full-blown kwashiorkor.

MARASMUS

Protein-energy malnutrition can lead to marasmus—one of the most serious forms of protein deficiency. This disease mainly affects children. The chances of developing this disease are high in children under the age of one. Generally, children living in developing countries are those most affected by this disease. However, children in developed countries can also be affected by it due to certain medical conditions. These medical complications can lead to the development of marasmus, even if the general factors causing marasmus are absent.

CAUSES

Marasmus can be caused by the deficiency of many nutrients. However, protein deficiency is its main cause. Contaminated water, poor diet, hunger, or inadequate food supply, can also lead to marasmus. Substituting breastfeeding with food items poor in nutrients can also cause marasmus in some cases. Cardiovascular diseases, genetic disorders, neurological problems, tuberculosis, or HIV infection can also create the conditions for the development of marasmus. Poverty is one of the most important ancillary causes of marasmus.

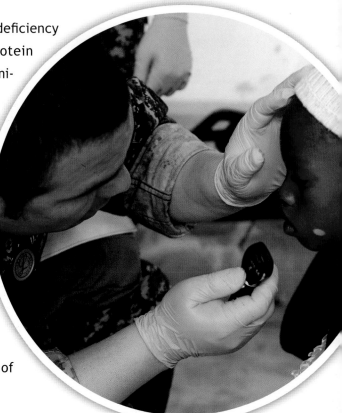

SYMPTOMS

There are many signs that help in detecting marasmus. Common symptoms of marasmus are weight loss, diarrhea, tiredness, loosening of skin, loss of muscle strength, and dryness of skin. In serious cases, vomiting and fainting may also occur. These symptoms may be visible daily or only occasionally, and can also vary according to the disease's condition and seriousness. In severe cases, the patient's head may also appear to be larger than the rest of the body.

PREVENTION

A healthy and nutritious diet is the key to a healthy body. Healthy eating also increases immunity. Mother's milk, carbohydrates, and proteins are very helpful. Sufficient quantity of food is also very important in the prevention of marasmus. Government authorities should play an active role in providing vulnerable communities with food benefits to help them achieve good health.

EFFECTS

Marasmus has many effects on the body, some of which are very serious in nature. This condition interferes with the normal physical growth of the body. The growth, development, and functioning of the nervous system, the endocrine system, the immune system, the cardiovascular system, the digestive system, and others, are also affected in this condition. In complicated cases, victims may even lose their eyesight and suffer from **deformity** of body parts.

TREATMENT

In mild cases, a properly developed nutrient-rich diet along with water consumption can help in improving the health of the patient. Medicated fluids, oral hydrating solutions, and feeding tubes are used in the treatment of complex cases of marasmus.

 DID YOU KNOW?

- Body weight can drop by 60 percent or more when someone has marasmus.
- The name *marasmus* comes from the Greek term for "withering."

VITAMIN-DEFICIENCY DISEASES

Our body needs a variety of vitamins for proper nourishment. Vitamins are essential for regulating the body's metabolism, developing body tissues and bones, and improving immunity. Vitamins can be broadly divided into six types: Vitamins A, C, D, E, K and B complex (a group of many vitamins). Poor diet, stress, medical problems, and limited sunlight—among others—can all cause certain vitamin deficiencies.

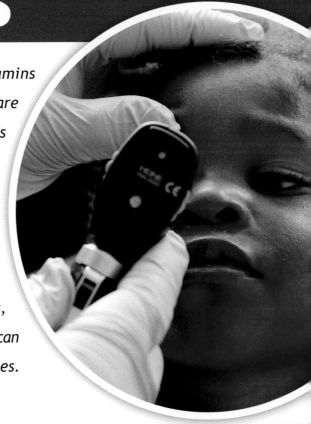

 WORDS TO UNDERSTAND

KERATOMALACIA: a rare eye disorder caused by a vitamin deficiency

NEUROLOGICAL: related to the brain and nervous system

OSTEOMALACIA: a condition involving the softening of bones

VITAMIN A DEFICIENCY

Vitamin A helps in the growth of body tissues, provides a smooth complexion, and reduces the chances of lung and oral cancers. It is very good for the health of eyes as well. The deficiency of Vitamin A can lead to night blindness, Bitot's spots, and **keratomalacia**. The skin can also become rough and dry. Consumption of food items rich in Vitamin A can help in preventing its deficiency. Dairy products, carrots, mango, and papaya are good sources of this vitamin.

VITAMIN B COMPLEX DEFICIENCY

Eight Vitamins—B1, B2, B3, B5, B6, B7, B9, and B12—combine to form the Vitamin B complex. They help in building a healthy nervous system, promoting cell growth, and keeping the skin and muscles healthy. However, their deficiency may lead to several health problems, such as muscular weakness, heart swelling, light sensitivity, diarrhea, sunburn, nausea, tiredness, and kidney stones.

DEFICIENCY OF VITAMINS E AND K

Vitamin E nourishes the body and cells and helps to prevent early aging. Vitamin E deficiency is rare. However, this deficiency can create some **neurological** problems and male infertility. Newborns can suffer from birth defects, such as an underdeveloped face, fingers, and other body parts, due to the deficiency of Vitamin K. It can also cause other problems like malfunctioning in bone formation, uncontrolled bleeding, and stomach problems.

DEFICIENCY OF VITAMIN C

Vitamin C is very important for our body. It improves immunity and also helps in building healthy bones and gums. It is very helpful in the process of wound healing. The deficiency of this vitamin can cause scurvy, and can also result in weakness, swollen gums, or nosebleeds. The chances of infections also increase due to decreased immunity caused by the deficiency of Vitamin C. Citrus fruits like oranges, lemons, and limes are good sources of Vitamin C.

DEFICIENCY OF VITAMIN D

Vitamin D is important for maintaining a healthy nervous system. It helps to strengthen the bones and teeth and is required for the absorption of calcium by the body. The deficiency of this vitamin can cause rickets in children. It can also cause **osteomalacia** in adults, which can lead to extreme deformity of bones. Natural sunlight is the best source of Vitamin D. Fish oil, butter, milk, and eggs are also good sources of Vitamin D.

 DID YOU KNOW?

- Vitamin C cannot be stored in the body, which makes its daily consumption important.
- The mildly insulting nickname for British people "limey" comes from British soldiers who consumed a lot of citrus juice to fight off scurvy.

MINERAL-DEFICIENCY DISEASES

Like all the other nutrients, minerals are also very important to maintain good health. Minerals are essential to help the body perform many functions related to growth and development. They help in producing energy, developing bones, and maintaining a healthy nervous system. Minerals are required by the body in varying quantities, but they can't be manufactured by the body—they must be absorbed from food. The five most important minerals to the human body are calcium, magnesium, phosphorous, potassium, and sodium. Other minerals that are essential are called trace minerals, and they include iodine, iron, and sulfur. Deficiency of these nutrients can cause health problems and lead to diseases.

WORDS TO UNDERSTAND

IODIZED: describes something (usually salt) that has had a small amount of iodine added to it

THYROID: a gland in the neck that produces hormones

TRACE: a very small amount

IODINE DEFICIENCY

This mineral plays a very important role in the developmental process. The deficiency of iodine interferes with the production of hormones in the **thyroid**. The deficiency of iodine can lead to thyroid disease with goiters, which involves a swelling in the neck. It can also lead to weight gain, weakness, dryness of skin, constipation, and even depression in some cases. Iodine deficiency in pregnant women can also cause birth defects in their unborn children. Iodine is mostly consumed through **iodized** salts.

IRON DEFICIENCY

The function of carrying oxygen from the lungs to the entire body is performed by iron. Iron deficiency can lead to anemia, a condition caused by the deficiency of hemoglobin in the blood. The deficiency of iron can affect many body parts. The ability of the body to perform many physical and mental tasks can also suffer due to this deficiency. Iron can be found in food items like green leafy vegetables, legumes, and cereals.

CALCIUM DEFICIENCY

Calcium is important for the formation and development of healthy bones and teeth. It also helps in the functioning of the blood-clotting system. People need good quantities of calcium throughout their lifetime. The deficiency of calcium can be of two types: dietary calcium deficiency and hypocalcemia. Dairy products, green vegetables, nuts, and cereals are rich sources of calcium. Vitamin D should be consumed along with a calcium-rich diet, as it helps in the absorption of calcium.

POTASSIUM DEFICIENCY

Healthy quantities of potassium in our body assist in the functioning of the heart, muscles, and kidneys. The deficiency of potassium can lead to blood pressure problems. It also affects bone health. Other signs and effects of potassium deficiency are tiredness, constipation, headache, depression, and heart problems. Strawberries, potatoes, apricots, tomatoes, oranges, and mangoes are some common sources of potassium.

ZINC DEFICIENCY

Many bodily functions depend on zinc. It is important for cell reproduction, improving fertility, and healing wounds. It also helps in improving the health of the immune system. Zinc deficiency can be identified from symptoms like sleep and behavior problems, hair loss, diarrhea, delay in wound healing, white spots on nails, and dry skin. Mild anemia may also be caused by zinc deficiency. Meat products, nuts, peas, eggs, and whole wheat grains are some sources of zinc.

 DID YOU KNOW?

- Magnesium can be found in whole grains, nuts, and leafy green vegetables.
- Overconsumption of zinc can disturb the absorption of copper by the body.

MALNUTRITION AND BRAIN HEALTH

Malnutrition affects the body's central nervous system, severely impacting the brain. The brain is in charge of thinking, emotions, and stimulating various functions of the human body. Lack of proteins, carbohydrates, fats, and micronutrients such as iodine, iron, folate, and others limits brain growth and slows down complex brain activities.

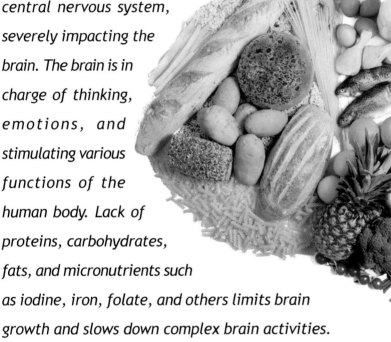

 ## WORDS TO UNDERSTAND

COGNITIVE: relating to the brain and thought
FETUS: a not-yet-born mammal
HINDERED: held back or interfered with

MALNUTRITION: THE BRAIN'S ENEMY

Insufficient intake of energy and nutrients affects the levels of chemicals in the brain called neurotransmitters. Neurotransmitters transmit nerve impulses from one nerve cell to another and influence mood, sleep patterns, and the thought process. Malnutrition can also damage nerves in the brain, causing changes in memory, hindering brain function and problem-solving ability.

MALNUTRITION AND YOUNG CHILDREN

Developing **fetuses** and young children are at a higher risk of brain damage from malnutrition. The brain grows at its fastest rate in the period from the conception of a baby to the time it turns three years old. This period, when the **cognitive** development of the brain might be boosted or **hindered**, is regarded as sensitive. Undernutrition during pregnancy can result in low birth weight, smaller head circumference, and reduced brain weight in newborns. Such children may be born blind, or deaf, or may have learning disabilities.

Find out more about the impact of nutrition on the body's metabolism.

CARBOHYDRATES AND MENTAL HEALTH

Carbohydrates significantly affect a person's mood and behavior. Carbohydrate-rich foods trigger the release of a hormone called insulin in the body. As insulin levels rise, more tryptophan enters the brain, which leads to increased production of the neurotransmitter serotonin. Higher serotonin levels in the brain enhance mood and have a sedating effect.

FATS AND MENTAL HEALTH

Intake of fats may also play a role in regulating mood and brain function. Studies suggest that lower levels of fat and cholesterol in the diet may reduce brain serotonin levels, causing mood changes, anger, and aggressive behavior.

STUNTING

Malnutrition during fetal development and early childhood can result in stunting. Stunted growth means reduced growth of height and weight according to age. The effects of stunting are permanent. Such children may never regain their height or weight. Stunting can also lead to premature death because vital organs never fully develop during childhood.

LONG-LASTING IMPACTS OF CHILDHOOD MALNUTRITION

Childhood malnutrition may cause problems in later years of life. According to a Chinese study, elderly men who experience childhood malnutrition have a 29 percent greater chance of cognitive impairment after the age of 65, while elderly women in the same age group are 35 percent more likely to have reduced brain function.

DID YOU KNOW?

- Iodine deficiency is a major cause of preventable birth defects.
- If pregnant women are deficient in folate, their babies are at increased risk of being born with a condition called spina bifida.

POVERTY AND MALNUTRITION

There are many factors that lead to malnutrition, but poverty is probably the most significant. Poverty creates conditions where people become incapable of having a nutritious diet. They are either forced to skip meals or settle for whatever is available to them. Choice does not play any role in their decisions related to food. Most cases of malnutrition are seen in poor countries or in low-income groups.

 WORDS TO UNDERSTAND

ALLEVIATE: ease or reduce

EXPENDITURE: spending

INDICATOR: a measure or gauge of something

DETERMINANTS OF POVERTY

Poverty is described as the inability to maintain the basic living standard. All the factors affecting the living standard help in judging whether poverty exists or not. The ability to maintain the basic income and **expenditure** level has a major effect on determining poverty. Other factors are regional and community-based **indicators**, such as availability of shelter. Reduced life expectancy, poor health, and illiteracy are some of the indirect results of poverty.

POVERTY & MALNUTRITION IN ASIA

Many Asian countries face the problem of poverty and malnutrition. South Asian countries like India, Pakistan, Bangladesh, Afghanistan, Bhutan, Nepal, and Sri Lanka register the highest cases of malnutrition. Most of these malnutrition problems are caused by poverty, since most of the countries in this continent are developing economies, and they have not yet been able to **alleviate** poverty and malnutrition completely.

POVERTY & MALNUTRITION IN AFRICA

African nations face serious poverty and malnutrition-related issues. The rate of poverty is increasing steadily in countries such as South Africa, Nigeria, Zimbabwe, and the sub-Saharan Africa region. Startlingly large numbers of Africans are believed to suffer from anemia. Other malnutrition problems such as night blindness, heart enlargement, and liver problems are also common in many parts. The soil in many African countries is also poor in iodine, making crops less nutritious.

POVERTY & MALNUTRITION IN OTHER COUNTRIES

Many Latin American, European, and Caribbean countries are also trying to eradicate poverty. Unequal distribution of income is the main cause of poverty in these countries. Food wastage is also very high in these nations.

MEASURES TAKEN TO REDUCE POVERTY

The government agencies of many countries have taken many measures to control the problem of poverty and malnutrition. Some poverty-reduction programs aim at raising the incomes of the poor, while others focus on reducing the impacts of the symptoms of poverty such as lack of housing, education, or medical care. Many laws related to food, education, shelter, and health have been passed for improving the living conditions of people suffering from poverty and malnutrition.

 DID YOU KNOW?

- Around 400 million people in the world don't have access to essential healthcare facilities.
- Millions of children die annually from preventable diseases due to insufficient levels of vaccination.

GLOBAL FOOD SITUATION

The world is facing a food crisis. According to estimates by the UN (United Nations), about 815 million people worldwide go hungry every day. Food prices are soaring, and the poorer sections of society are unable to afford food. Food production also faces challenges due to lack of irrigation facilities and changing climate patterns. These factors have led to the deepening of the food crisis. Effective policies and immediate action are now required to deal with this crisis.

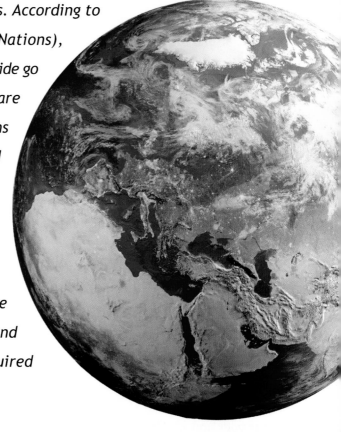

 ## WORDS TO UNDERSTAND

BIOFUELS: alternative energy sources made from living things such as plants

ERRATIC: unpredictable

REGULATED: controlled by government policy

ASIA'S EFFECT ON THE GLOBAL FOOD SITUATION

The policies and attitudes of many Asian countries like India, Pakistan, China, and Vietnam have negatively affected the global food market. The global supply of food grains is disturbed by several strict policies imposed by these nations. Export of food grains has been banned in many countries, and the prices are also strictly regulated. This has led to an increase in food prices throughout the world. Many political and economic factors involved in formulating the food policies of the Asian countries also create food uncertainties.

AMERICA'S EFFECT ON THE GLOBAL FOOD SITUATION

The United States engages in the production of many biofuels. Food products like corn, soybeans, and sugarcane are commonly used for making such fuels. This is a positive step in that biofuels reduce the nation's dependency on foreign oil. However, biofuels have a downside: they increase food shortages in the world because the crops are used to generate fuel for automobiles instead of being fed to the hungry.

DISPARITIES IN FOOD PRODUCTION

While the overall production of food has increased over the years, problems have been experienced in its distribution. Records also show that the developed countries are producing more food grains than the developing countries. In fact, countries like the United States and Canada are growing more food crops than Africa, even though more land in Africa is under cultivation than in North America.

IMPACT OF CLIMATE CHANGE

Food production is affected by climatic changes. The increasing levels of carbon dioxide in the atmosphere and the changing climate patterns pose a threat to the growth of crops across the world. The yield suffers and so does the food supply. In many countries, erratic rainfall leads to the damage of food crops. Production of food reduces in harsh climatic conditions. This increases food prices, later creating a number of other food problems.

Find out how climate change will impact our food supply.

SOLVING FOOD PROBLEMS

Food problems are not only emerging because of shortage but also due to waste. Investment in irrigation, regular soil testing, formulating effective food laws, extending more credit to farmers, proper marketing in developing countries, and developing storage facilities are required to deal with the world's enormous food problems. It is the responsibility of governments to treat the issues related to food production as a priority.

DID YOU KNOW?

- Only 2.5 percent or the world's water is fresh water.
- The acidification of ocean waters due to carbon dioxide is harmful to marine life.

WATER PROBLEMS

The world's food problems can be aggravated by problems surrounding consumable water. Water is an extremely important part of our food and our lives. Almost 75 percent of the Earth's surface is covered with water. However, only 2.5 percent of it can be used for consumption, as the remaining water is saline. Much of that fresh water is locked up in Antarctica in the form of glaciers. For all practical purposes, only 0.5 percent of the total water on Earth is available for consumption.

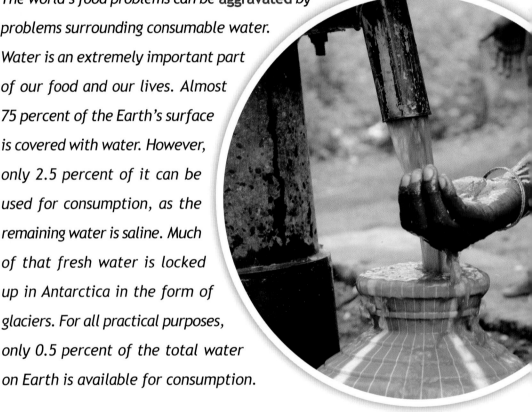

 ## WORDS TO UNDERSTAND

AGGRAVATED: made worse

CONTAMINATION: the act of making something impure or toxic

DESALINIZATION: a process of removing the salt from water

THE WATER SITUATION

As the water available to us is limited, its increased use over time has caused many problems. Fresh water is found in rivers, lakes, and snow. Rainwater is also a source of freshwater. The availability of this water is maintained through the water cycle. However, due to increased use, our water resources are declining at a quick pace. Glaciers are melting quicker than expected, and the water table is dropping every year due to global warming. These developments pose a serious threat to the world.

WATER IN INDUSTRIES

The industrial sector also requires water for many uses. After agriculture, industries are believed to be the largest consumers of water. The most common use of water in industries is as a cooling agent in power plants. Water is used for direct power generation as well. Other industries like sugar mills, textiles, paper mills, pharmaceuticals, and others also use water. Many industries also use water as a medium to dispose of waste.

WATER & FOOD SECURITY

Large-scale food production is required to meet the world's food requirements. Water is used in great quantities to irrigate the crops. Droughts and floods create major food problems throughout the world. A stable food-production system can be maintained only through proper water management. Climatic changes also affect food problems, because many countries depend on rainfall for irrigation. Many irrigation techniques and methods have been developed to deal with the water problems surrounding food production.

HUMAN CONTRIBUTION TO WATER PROBLEMS

There are many ways through which human beings contribute to the water problems of the world. Leakage in water distribution systems, inefficient use of water in agriculture and industries, and **contamination** of fresh water sources are just some of the ways that water resources are being disturbed. Excess water quantities are also withdrawn from underground sources, increasing the world's water problems.

SOLVING WATER PROBLEMS

Many efforts are being made to solve the world's water problems. **Desalinization** technology has emerged as the biggest solution, as most water resources are wasted due to the salinity of water. This technology has been successful in many countries of North Africa and the Middle East. Preserving existing resources through proper use in all possible forms could be the best solution to water problems.

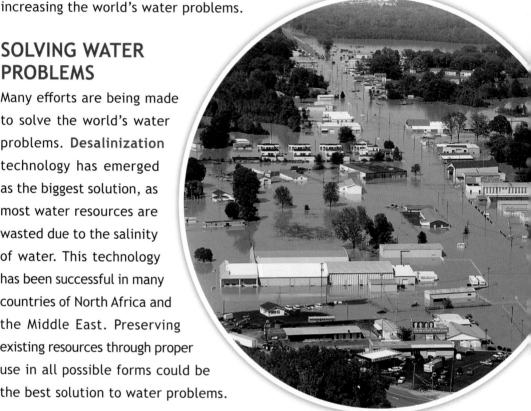

DID YOU KNOW?

- Asian rivers are the most polluted rivers in the world.
- A substantial number of diseases in developing countries are caused by contaminated water.

THE SAHEL CRISIS

The Sahel region is an impoverished area of Africa where millions of people are affected by hunger. About 20 million people in the Sahel region are affected by food insecurity, of which 3 million are children. More than 1 million children under five are suffering from acute malnutrition and another 1.9 million suffer from moderate malnutrition.

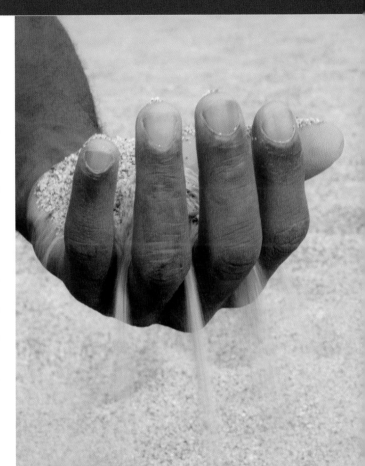

 ## WORDS TO UNDERSTAND

ACUTE: severe
CYCLIC: recurring regularly

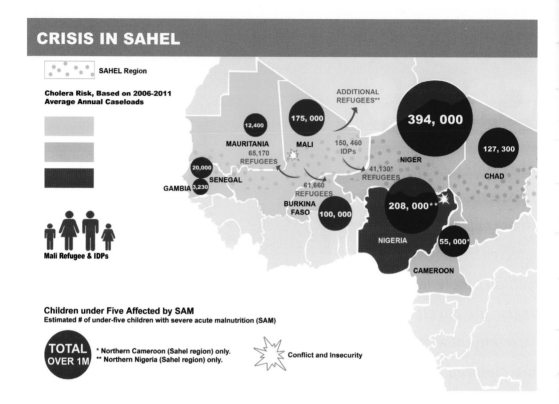

CRISIS IN SAHEL

SAHEL Region

Cholera Risk, Based on 2006-2011
Average Annual Caseloads

ADDITIONAL
REFERGEES**

12,400

175,000

394,000

MAURITANIA
65,170
REFUGEES

MALI

150,460
IDPs

127,300

20,000

41,130*
REFUGEES

NIGER

CHAD

GAMBIA 3,230

SENEGAL

61,660
REFUGEES

BURKINA
FASO 100,000

208,000**

NIGERIA

55,000*

Mali Refugee & IDPs

CAMEROON

Children under Five Affected by SAM
Estimated # of under-five children with severe acute malnutrition (SAM)

TOTAL
OVER 1M

* Northern Cameroon (Sahel region) only.
** Northern Nigeria (Sahel region) only.

Conflict and Insecurity

THE SAHEL BELT

The Sahel belt cuts across Africa from the Atlantic Ocean to the Red Sea, including countries such as Niger, Chad, Burkina Faso, Mali, Mauritania, Nigeria, Senegal, Sudan, and Cameroon. The situation of malnutrition in these countries is serious. The incidence of Global **Acute** Malnutrition (GAM) in these countries, except Cameroon, equals or exceeds 10 percent. GAM prevalence in Chad and many regions of Niger and Mauritania has surpassed the emergency level of 15 percent.

THE UNDERLYING PROBLEM

Cyclic droughts lead to poor harvests, which in turn lead to price increases, and are the underlying problem of the Sahel region. This limits the ability of people to buy food. To survive in difficult times, families have no other option but to compromise on the quantity and quality of food. According to the organizations operating there, the main reason for chronic malnutrition in the Sahel region is not drought or food deficit but the ever-increasing rise in food prices.

MALNUTRITION AND INFECTIOUS DISEASES

Malnourished people have a weak immune system and are more susceptible to infectious diseases, which further lowers the nutritional status of the affected person. This creates a vicious cycle of malnutrition and disease. Additionally, the lack of effective systems to address the nutritional, health, water, and sanitation needs of people creates a serious threat to life in the Sahel belt. Most of the population have limited access to affordable curative and preventive health services.

HIGH-RISK POPULATIONS

Malnutrition poses the greatest risk to young children, pregnant women, and nursing mothers, as they have special nutritional needs. At least 35 percent of all child deaths in the Sahel belt every year occur due to acute malnutrition and severe acute malnutrition.

WHAT WORSENS THE SAHEL CRISIS?

Food crisis has severe effects on families. In many cases, food insecurity leads to early marriages, when families marry off their daughters so that they don't have to feed them. Risks of maternal deaths and complications during childbirth are common. People may force their children to drop out of school to work so that they can supplement the family income. Boys are sent to beg in the streets, and girls may get involved in petty trading or domestic work to support their families. These children lose their childhood at an early age, become parents, have children, and the cycle continues. Additionally, the conflict over scarce resources may increase tensions and violence between various communities.

DID YOU KNOW?

- The Sahel region experiences the greatest increases in food insecurity in the world.
- The number of children suffering from malnutrition saw a 50 percent increase between 2017 and 2018.

TEXT-DEPENDENT QUESTIONS

- What is malnutrition?
- What are the effects of malnutrition on the body?
- What are potential social and economic effects of malnutrition?
- What is the impact of hunger on the elderly?
- What is "the right to food"?
- What are some symptoms of starvation?
- What are some examples of local food systems?
- What is the difference between primary and secondary malnutrition?
- What are some important mineral-deficiency diseases?
- Where is the Sahel and what is happening there?

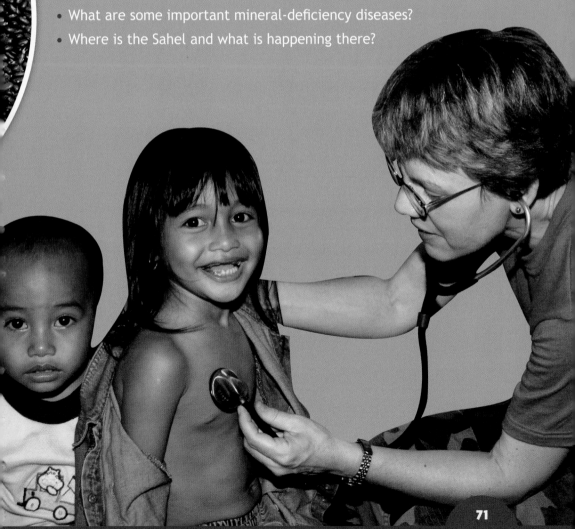

- Imagine that you have a friend who is suffering from malnutrition. Using the information in this book and outside sources, plan a week's worth of meals that will make sure your friend is eating a healthy, balanced diet.
- Find out about hunger and malnutrition in your community. There is probably a local food bank and/or community kitchen somewhere near you. Ask them what they need and how you can help out, such as collecting canned goods for a pantry or helping serve meals at a shelter.
- Choose a key part of a healthy diet, such as protein or minerals. Find out more about it and what foods are good sources. Then do something with what you've learned, such as creating a poster to educate others or, if you like to cook, preparing a meal that shows off what you've studied.
- Find out more about the Sahel crisis and what international relief organizations are doing to try and ease the problems there. Select an organization, such as CARE (Cooperative for Assistance and Relief Everywhere), Oxfam, Mercy Corps, or UNHCR (United Nations High Commissioner for Refugees) and write a report on what they are doing.

amino acid: an organic molecule that is the building block of proteins.

antibody: a protein in the blood that fights off substances the body thinks are dangerous.

antioxidant: a substance that fights against free radicals, molecules in the body that can damage other cells.

biofortification: the process of improving the nutritional value of crops through breeding or genetic modification.

calories: units of heat used to indicate the amount of energy that foods will produce in the human body.

carbohydrates: substances found in certain foods (such as bread, rice, and potatoes) that provide the body with heat and energy and are made of carbon, hydrogen, and oxygen.

carcinogen: something that causes cancer.

cardiovascular: of or relating to the heart and blood vessels.

carnivorous: meat-eating.

cholesterol: a soft, waxy substance present in all parts of the body, including the skin, muscles, liver, and intestines.

collagen: a fibrous protein that makes up much of the body's connective tissues.

deficiency: a lack of something, such as a nutrient in one's diet.

derivative: a product that is made from another source; for example, malt comes from barley, making it a barley derivative.

diabetes: a disease in which the body's ability to produce the hormone insulin is impaired.

dietary supplements: products taken orally that contain one or more ingredient (such as vitamins or amino acids) that are intended to supplement one's diet and are not considered food.

electrolytes: substances (such as sodium or calcium) that are ions in the body regulating the flow of nutrients into and waste products out of cells.

enzyme: a protein that starts or accelerates an action or process within the body.

flexible: applies to something that can be readily bent, twisted, or folded without any sign of injury.

food additive: a product added to a food to improve flavor, appearance, nutritional value, or shelf life.

genetically modified organism (GMO): a plant or animal that has had its genetic material altered to create new characteristics.

growth hormone: a substance either naturally produced by the body or synthetically made that stimulates growth in animals or plants.

herbicide: a substance designed to kill unwanted plants, such as weeds.

hydration: to supply with ample fluid or moisture.

macronutrients: nutrients required in large amounts for the health of living organisms, including proteins, fats, and carbohydrates.

metabolism: the chemical process by which living cells produce energy.

micronutrients: nutrients required in very small amounts for the health of living organisms.

nutritional profile: the nutritional makeup of given foods, including the balance of vitamins, minerals, proteins, fats, and other components.

obesity: a condition in which excess body fat has amassed to the point where it causes ill-health effects.

pasteurization: a process that kills microorganisms, making certain foods and drinks safer to consume.

pesticide: a substance designed to kill insects or other organisms that can cause damage to plants or animals.

processed food: food that has been refined before resale, often with additional fats, sugars, sodium, and other additives.

protein: a nutrient found in food (as in meat, milk, eggs, and beans) that is made up of many amino acids joined together, is a necessary part of the diet, and is essential for normal cell structure and function.

protein complementation: the dietary practice of combining different plant-based foods to get all of the essential amino acids.

refined: when referring to grains or flours, describing those that have been processed to remove elements of the whole grain.

sustainable: a practice that can be successfully maintained over a long period of time.

vegan: a person who does not eat meat, poultry, fish, dairy, or other products sourced from animals.

vegetarian: a person who does not eat meat, poultry, or fish.

whole grain: grains that have been minimally processed and contain all three main parts of the grain—the bran, the germ, and the endosperm.

workout: a practice or exercise to test or improve one's fitness for athletic competition, ability, or performance.

FURTHER READING

Lappe, Francis Moore, and Joseph Collins. *World Hunger: 10 Myths*. New York: Grove, 2018.

Newby, P.K. *Food and Nutrition: What Everyone Needs to Know*. New York: Oxford University Press, 2018.

Sahn, David E. *The Fight Against Hunger and Malnutrition*. New York and Oxford, UK: Oxford University Press, 2015.

Tappan, Jennifer. *The Riddle of Malnutrition*. Athens: Ohio University Press, 2017.

INTERNET RESOURCES

CARE: GLOBAL HUNGER CRISIS

Find out about world hunger from the anti-poverty charity, CARE.

https://www.care.org/emergencies/global-hunger-crisis

GLOBAL NUTRITION REPORT

Annual report issued by the World Health Organization.

https://globalnutritionreport.org/

NUTRITION FOR KIDS

Find out more about young people's nutritional needs.

https://www.mayoclinic.org/healthy-lifestyle/childrens-health/in- depth/nutrition-for-kids/art-20049335

WORLD HUNGER FACTS

Data about global hunger from the Grameen Foundation.

https://www.freedomfromhunger.org/world-hunger-facts

INDEX

Photo Credits

Photographs sourced by Macaw Media, except for the following:
Cover and pg. 1: © fneun | Shutterstock, © VGstockstudio | Shutterstock, © Morakod1977 | Shutterstock, © Milles Studio | Shutterstock, © XiXinXing | Shutterstock, © Kseniya Tatarnikova | Shutterstock, © Milles Studio | Shutterstock; pg. 7: © Lenazajchikova | Dreamstime, © Ro©n Mackenzie | Dreamstime, © Angel Luis Simon Martin | Dreamstime | Shutterstock; pg. 9: © AlinaMD | Shutterstock; pg. 10: © Milles Studio; pg. 12: © Billion Photos | Shutterstock; pg. 14: © Valentyn75 | Dreamstime, © Mallivan | Dreamstime; pg. 15: © Loonara | Dreamstime; pg. 20: © Kouassi Gilbert Ambeu | Dreamstime; pg. 21: © Dofoto | Dreamstime; pg. 38: © Rawpixel.com | Shutterstock; pg. 39: © Joshua Resnick | Shutterstock; pg. 50: © Belier | Dreamstime; pg. 52: © pathdoc | Shutterstock; pg. 53: © Ilka-erika Szasz-fabian | Dreamstime; pg. 55: © Tijanap | Dreamstime; pg. 56: © pathdoc | Shutterstock; pg. 60: © Sergey Mayorov | Dreamstime; pg. 61: © 7xpert | Dreamstime; pg. 64: © Gnanamclicks | Dreamstime; pg. 67: © DiversityStudio1 | Dreamstime; pg. 70: © Davide Bonaldo | Dreamstime; pg. 73: © Riccardo Lennart Niels Mayer | Dreamstime